I'm

Grateful

for

You